KEITH LEMON:

THE RULES

KEITH LEMON:

THE RULES

69 WAYS TO BE SUCCE~~SS~~FUL ^SEX

Keith Lemon is a northern sex symbol. If you don't know already it's the same Keith Lemon as Keith Lemon Business Man of the Year 1993. You may have seen him on TV on such shows as Celebrity Juice, A Bear's Tail, Bo Selecta, Bo in the USA or Keith Lemon's Very Brilliant World Tour. As you can see he's a good looking guy and a big hit with the ladies – from bang tidy lasses to stinky mingers, he's had them all!

Fanks

I'd like to say fanks to allt people that helped me make this book: me agent, the publishers, you (for buying it!) but most of all the fine super bang ladies that have given me all the experienceses that I've experienced. Without you this book wouldn't have been possible, and I wouldn't have been able to help people become a fanny magnet like meself. Fank you, and free Melson Nandela! Ooooooosh!

CONTENTS

STYLE

THE BREEDING GROUND

ONLINE

BANTER

ONE NIGHTSTANDS

FIRST DATES

SEX

46. Put on a DVD to get you in t' mood
47. Learn how to turn a woman on
48. Try an aphrodisiac
49. Pick your venue carefully
50. Keep it spicy
51. Choke the chicken as often as you need to
52. Have some sexy phone sex
53. Always use protection

RELATIONSHIPS

54. Treat em mean and keep em keen
55. Never get caught eyeing up another girl
56. Meet her mates - if she's tidy, they will be too
57. Avoid meeting the parents for at least two weeks
58. Keep calm and win the minge
59. Always notice a new haircut
60. Avoid the painters
61. Understand what they mean when they say...
62. Never forget a Valentine's Day card
63. Celebrate Valentine's Day in style
64. Remember to buy regular gifts
65. If it isn't working out, get rid
66. Get two tellies
67. Never reveal the number
68. Maintain your independence
69. If you get dumped go on t' rebound

OUTRO

WHAT HAVE YOU LEARNT?

HOW DO!
My name

You might've seen me on't telly (I host a quiz called 'Celebrity Juice' with two bang tidy birds – Holly Willoughbooby and Fearne Cotton – who pretends to hate me, but there's real passion in her eyes), or in't street, or in Costco, or at a nightclub dancing probably better than Jamiroquai. If you're a girl, you've probably seen me in yer dreams.

Anyway, I've got too much love in my body for one woman at the moment – I'm riding a lady wave. Sometimes I feel like Rocky but instead of kids following me when I'm out training or walking t' shop, it's women. So I thought I'd share my secrets with you so you can be like me and be a succ-sex.

Follow my 69 rules to find out how to dress to impress, where to go, what to say and how

is Keith Lemon.

to do it. There're even some tips for all those bang tidy lasses out there too – look out for the lady symbol. There's only 69 ways, but I'll give you 70 to a 100 in't next book if I do one. Also 69 is funny i'nt it? Cos its like that sex act that's upside down sort off where he has a go on her whilst she's having a go on him. Oooooosh!

The book is splattered with a array of colourful pictures so if you can't read you can look at them. Plus there is a few phone numbers in here of girls that I've had a right good time with if for some reason you can't get any action after reading this. But I'm sure you will as you're learning from the minge master himself!

see p.128. Kelli is well fit.

OK, let's get this party bus on the road and let's commence!

All t'gest
Keith Lemon

some birds knickers wot were thrown at me in the street

11

STYLE

This category is all about style: who has it and how you can get it.

Style is as important as the tiny arms on a T-Rex. Although I'm not sure what they were for cos they look like they cun't do owt. But I'm sure they were there for a reason. I prefer diplodocus anyway, if you were to ask me what me favourite dinosaur was.

Anywhere, without style you are not stylish. Style puts you into different mating sectors (sectORs). Your style predicts what collective you are apart of. It's what's on the outside that will decide if you get inside, if ya know what I mean.

#1 KEEP YOUR PULLING APPARATUS FINELY TUNED

1. Exercise daily with 3 hours of swingball.

3. Visit the dentist every 6 months and the hairdressers every 6 weeks.

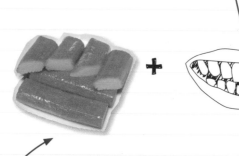

2. Eat healthy. Crab sticks have no fat content in them. Only have one kebab a week otherwise you'll be carrying more timber than a pork scratching.

4. Don't spend too long on any game console – it will suck your personality out of your heart. Don't use facespace, pagebook or tweeter too much. Speak to real people that exist in real life.

6. Learn a new word every day. Here's one for ya that I just learned: 'ubiquitous'. It means that something is everywhere. Like if you go to Magaluf the fanny is ubiquitous!

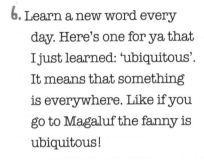

biliry.
ubiquitous (ūbik´witəs) *a.* **1** present everywhere or in an indefinite number of places at the same time. **2** frequently encountered. **ubiquitously** *adv.* **ubiquitousness, ubiquity** *n.*
-uble (ūbəl) *suf.* that can or must be, as

5. Choke the chicken at least once a day. Tell yourself in the mirror that you are bang tidy and you'd love to smash your own back doors in.

These are just a few simple rules to keep your finely tuned pulling apparatus finely tuned. Your body and mind is a temple look after it right nicely.

#2 IF YOU'RE NOT FIT, DRESS UP AS SOMEONE WHO IS

The rules of attraction are simple. You have to be attractive. Some people aren't attractive, so what do they do? They dress up as somebody who is.

To some men style comes easy, like me. Whether I'm in a linen suit or leather trousers, I always look stylish. My look is inspired by different style icons fused with my own sense of fashion.

Take a look at the diagram on the right to see how I achieve my own look. Get a few of these items in yer wardrobe and you'll be heading in t' right direction.

Moustache: Keep it tidy and the girls'll love the extra tickle

Necklace: Not a girly one, a shark's tooth. You'll be like Crocodile Dundee, but sharks not crocs

Leather trousers: She won't be able to resist a feel

Snakeskin shoes: Shows you don't mind splashing the cash

And for all the lasses, see over t' page.

Bikini top: optional

Bikini bottoms: optional

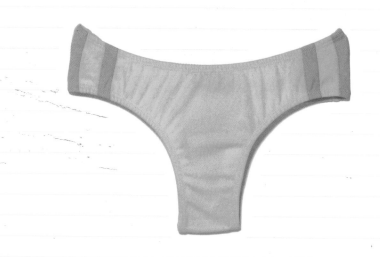

Another fella to look to for inspiration is Hollywood actor Owen Wilson. I have a lot of respect for him. He wears right summery suits. Got great hair too. That's a nice cream jacket, it looks money that. Only thing he's missing here is a whale's tooth accessory. That'd finish off this smart casual look right off. Take your Jennifer Aniston look-a-like totty to somewhere nice like Nando's then back to yours for some hot n' spicy reggae reggae source all over t' face! Ooooosh!

tallywacker

Tip: This would work much better if he had a whale's tooth

If I had to gay off with a man cos me life depended on it then it would be Owen. That's not to say that I've ever fought about it before. One of me mates asked me that once. 'If I had to gay off with a man who would it be?' I fought it was a bit of a strange question. It was even strangerer when he said the man he'd gay off with would be me. He also said that when he has a masturbate he sometimes sticks his thumb up his crack.

Anywhere, the only thing that's wrong with Owen Wilson is that he's got a nose like a tallywacker. He could take that hooter for a piss. You'd fink that with all his Hollywood spondulex he'd get his nose fixed and get rid of the bell end on't end. Same with her from 'Sex in't City' with the wart on her chin. I call her nipple chin.

nipple chin

#3 WEAR BLACK TO SCULPT YOUR BODY

Unless you are a hormone sexual like me brother, you may not be familiar with top hairdresser, Nicky Clarke. Another very stylish man who I know simply because I'm on telly and this is the kind of people you bump into when you go to show biz bashesses (yes it's true I do know Myleene Class and I have smashed her back doors in at a function).

But anywhere, Nicky Clarke must be in his 50s and he still looks young. He knows the rule: wear black to define your figure. It's also great for hiding timber especially if you have a beer belly, its very slimming – not that Nicky needs that.

Maybe he's me dad

0
0
0

#4 STRUT LIKE YOU'RE A WILD BOY

You've got the look, now you've got to own it. If you can't carry it off, you'll look like a right nonce. 'Wild Boy' is a great tune to have in your head as you strut. If you don't know what strutting is let me tell ya – walking with a swagger. Pick a tune in your head and walk to that beat, stride with rhythm, it looks good. In fact, Simon le Bon is another stylish man. He's roughly in his 60s but he looks like he's just walked straight out of River Island, and that in't an easy look to pull off at that age. Again, he's got good hair which can often decide what clothes you should wear. Blond, or if like me strawberry blond, can mainly be worn with almost any colour. That's why gingers always look like geeks cos their orange hair doesn't go with owt. Poor buggers.

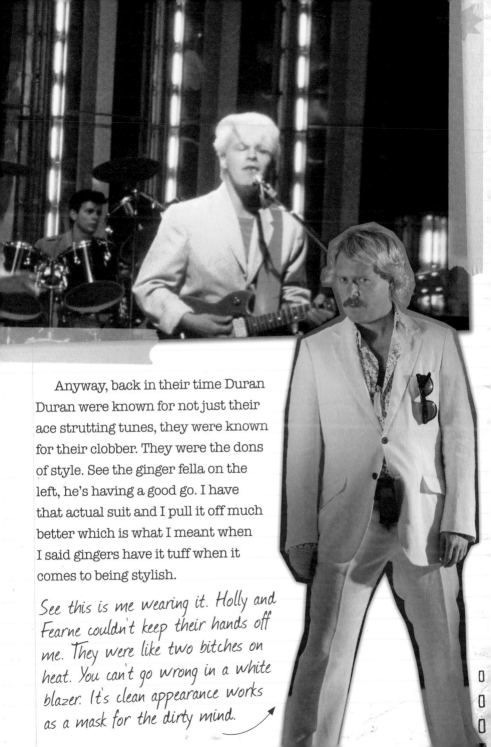

Anyway, back in their time Duran Duran were known for not just their ace strutting tunes, they were known for their clobber. They were the dons of style. See the ginger fella on the left, he's having a good go. I have that actual suit and I pull it off much better which is what I meant when I said gingers have it tuff when it comes to being stylish.

See this is me wearing it. Holly and Fearne couldn't keep their hands off me. They were like two bitches on heat. You can't go wrong in a white blazer. It's clean appearance works as a mask for the dirty mind.

Turning your tallywacker the same colour as the Incredible Hulk isn't going to do you any favours

#5 BRUSH AND FLOSS EVERYDAY

It might seem like a ball ache but you should always brush yer teeth and floss each day – no one is going to be kissing you if you smell like something died in yer mouth. Maybe even use mouthwash. But always spit it out. I heard a rumour that if you swallow it it can make your tallywacker go green, pink or blue depending what colour yer mouthwash is.

#6 GET A SUN-KISSED GLOW

I like to look like I've just come back from me holidays. So apply fake tan to give that sun-kissed glow. It'll make you look healthier and more virile even if you've eaten nothing but fried chicken and not seen sunlight for a month.

Lucky for me, I carry the black jean from my dad's side so just one can of fake tan can last me a whole three years. My mum said that she had an affair with Billy Ocean and it could be possible that he is me dad.

If you go to a salon and get a spray, it's a good idea to take a colour chart with you, or try one of the following:

'I'll have a Dale Winton please'

'Can I try a Katie Price this time?'

'I'm off to Tenerife so I'll go David Dickenson please'

Take this handy chart to your tanning salon and get exact same colour as your fav celeb.

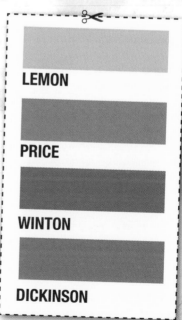

LEMON

PRICE

WINTON

DICKINSON

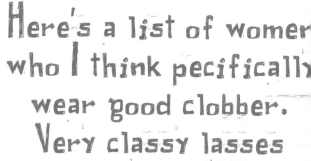

Here's a list of women who I think pecifically wear good clobber. Very classy lasses

Poudre de Martin

USE AFTER T'BATH

200g NET

*BE INSPIRED BY THE GREATS: MARTIN MCCUTCHEON.

She's got a boy's name but just look at that... perfect beach attire. She knows how to dress to make the most of her assets – we can all learn from that. I can just imagine un-tying those bikini bottoms with me teeth! If you get the lads thinking that, you're in.

I've met Martin, she smells a bit like talc. Hey I talc meself, it stops me from getting a sweaty bum. Nowt wrong with a talccer! She looks bang on those ads for little bottles of milk where she's on about giving your body some T.L.C. I'd give her some T.L.C. Some tender Lemon cuddles!

*BE INSPIRED BY THE GREATS: JODIE MARSH

To me, Jodie Marsh is a fashion icon. The way she revolutionised the belt by utilising it as a bra top was bloody brilliant. I just think it's so creative. She could wear it at a club or on't red carpet later in't evening, and she's showing just enough boobage to let you know she's got nice bangers, yer don't after imagine owt. It's all there for yer to see, whilst still not showing too much. And then she glammed it up and turned it into a wedding gown. What a beautiful bride she makes. And what happened after that? She turned into a lesbican. An amazingly fit lesbican! Not sure if she's still a bean flicker but if she is 'Jodie giza call'. Love fit lesbicans.

She's got a great colour about her too. The colour of a hot dog! One of me favourite foods.

Look, perfect match!

I'd take her up the aisle!

*BE INSPIRED BY THE GREATS: CLAIRE SWEENEY

And who could forget about Claire Sweeney. I've had a thing for her for many years. Totally different to Martin and Jodie but never the less always well turned out. Propper classy like… she's a right woman. I don't know what it is but she has it. Really stylish bird. Knows how to wear a hat as well. Bang tidy.

You can't just learn style like mine and Claire's, but try out a few of these rules and you'll be giving it a good go. If you're a girl that looks like any of these ladies I'd love to meet you. Or if Louise Rednapp ever gets divorced, call me.

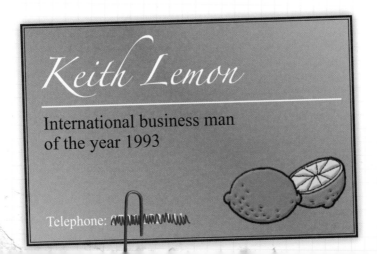

Keith Lemon

International business man
of the year 1993

Telephone:

Knows how to wear a hat

Classy not trashy

#7 IT'S NEVER TOO HOT TO WEAR LEATHER

Ladies love a man in leather trousers and fellas like women in leather hot pants. Remember it is never too hot to wear leather trousers. I've got two pairs cos you can't wash 'em. You just after air them out. It's like having a tap up ya crack.

#8 MAKE SURE YOU MATCH YOUR SHOES TO YOUR OUTFIT

Women often judge a man by his shoes. Which is a bit daft, but to be on safe side always make sure your shoes complement the rest of what you're wearing. White snake skin shoes seem to always impress.

#9 LOOK AFTER YOUR LOCKS AND THEY'LL LOOK AFTER YOU

fig 1. Le Bon

fig 2. Wilson

fig 3. Clarke

he knows it

As I've said Owen Wilson, Nicky Clarke, Le Bon and Rick Parfitt they all have good hair. Don't wear it too long so you look like you're in Status Quo but it's nice to have a bit of length so your lover can run their fingers through it as they reach climax. Him out of status quo must have seen me on telly. Seems to have sorted his bonce out now. He looks good. Maybe he's my dad. Keep reading to find out! All will be revealed ... Oooosh!

#10 KEEP YOUR FEET PINE FRESH

If you have problems with stinky feet leave one of those magic tree air freshners in each shoe over night. Will keep them smelling like a fresh woodland forest!

FEET Fresh

FEET Fresh

THE BREEDING GROUND

In this bit I will give you some tips on places to pull. You'll never be a minge magnet or a cock conqueror if you're in the wrong place. Get off facespace and tweeter and get out there and meet people. There's no such thing as 'all dressed up and no where to go'. If you're dressed up get out there and go. Where you fink might be the right place to meet someone might not be the right place to meet someone. So let me tell yer where is and where isn't. If you already knew you wouldn't be sat at home. Come on, I'll tell yer where to meet folk.

#11 ALWAYS HUNT IN PACKS

First off, make sure your pulling partner is a bit of a munter – that way you'll look even more attractiverer. What I always find works is just to stand in the corner and start laughing with yer mate over nowt. Eventually you'll catch somebody's eye and when they clock you pissing yourself laughing with your mate they'll think – 'Hey they look fun, I wish I was having as much fun as them'. Apologise as you're laughing and say 'Sorry, I'm not laughing at you.'

Where's that rabbit? I'm gonna destroy it.

And this is where your banter skills come into play. You'll
need a story to tell that's just made you laugh, something like
'My mate has just showed me a picture of his dog dressed as
superman having it off with a rabbit, he's crazy!' Crazy but
not mad. People don't like mad people unless they're mad
themselves. Mad bastards. Think you know what I mean.

#12 PERFECT YOUR SIGNATURE DANCE

Clubs are the classic breeding ground as it's dark, everyone is pissed and if you're a good dancer like me then basically your moves are a mating call. If you want to play things a bit cooler, I always find a good launch into a Russian dance works. Girls are amazed by it.

fig 1.

fig 2.

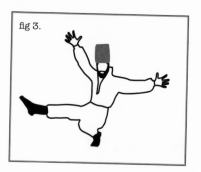

fig 3.

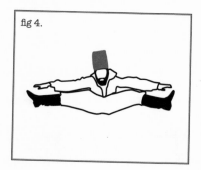

fig 4.

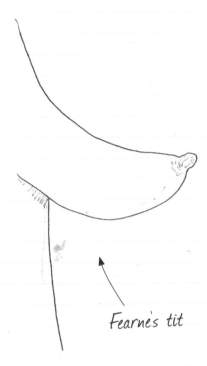

Fearne's tit

But be aware your legs will hurt the next morning like you've run a marathon. Like what Fearne Cotton did. Only not because she couldn't even be arsed to do a full 'n. I'm only joking, she does a lot of work for charity does Nostrils. She'd eat a dog shit sandwich if she thought it was gonna raise some money for someone. Heart of gold. Tits of a boy.

If you want to be a bit more suggestive, I like to dance behind a girl and basically do a body shake. It really turns them on. I call this the body shake.

OOOOSH!

#13 YOUR PULLING RADAR SHOULD BE ON AT ALL TIMES

You never know when you're gonna walk round the corner and bump into a nest of bang tidy totty so you should always be prepared. Think about other places – hospital waiting rooms for one. People are often emotional wrecks and are always looking for guidance. Like little bambis on ice. I've pulled enough birds in hospitals. Even patients! If they're not into you at first, they can't escape if they're in bed tied up to a drip so you've got plenty of time to win them over. Plus you can check out what they look like without make-up on. If they look fit when they're ill with no make-up on, imagine what they look like when they've got a face full of slap on! Super bang!

Doesn't have to be patients, she's asking for it

Hold up your end!

I've shown a few who's the daddy

(BUT I'm not the real daddy and I'll do a D&A test on Jeremy Kyle to prove it)

#14 VISIT SOFT PLAY AREAS TO SECURE THE YUMMY MUMMY

They're those places that look like catalogue warehouses but inside its full of mums with their kids swinging about and jumping into ball pools. Borrow a mate's kid and take it out there for an afternoon. There's always a milf there waiting for the right man to come along and play dad.

WARNING this is no place for a shag and run. Only go here if you wanna take on the responsibility of looking after kids, or yer really desperate.

OOOOOSH!

#15 SUPERMARKET SWEEP LIKE MEL GIBSON

In 'Lethal Weapon 2', Mel Gibson showed us that it's easy to pull in a supermarket. Look out for the scene where he's trying it on with Patsy Kensit (who I know in real life). He simply gives her some advice when she pics up a melon. Tells her to pick one from the bottom as they put the old stock on top. Straight off she's impressed by his knowledge of melons (banter). Then he asks her to have dinner with him she says no, but he persists and tells her 'Be original say yes, everyone else says no' (great banter). Then he pokes her in the eyes and says he's a gourmet cook. Never poke a girl in the eyes, that's a bit odd. But he keeps at it and pretends she's stealing his shopping basket (again a bit odd) but before you know they're back in his caravan on't beach. I fink he gets it twice. Ya see her bangers too! Of course I've seen them in real life. She's as fit now as she was back then!

Breeding

Still bang tidy

Fancy a ride?

OOOOOSH!

HERE'S MY WEEKLY SHOPPING LIST

When some fit lass clocks these items in your trolley, she knows what a stud you are. You'll be gobbled off in the car park before you have time to load your groceries into the boot of your car.

Bumped in to Michelle in the fruit isle at Morrisons last week so I popped a couple of right ripe plums in her basket!

COSTO

SHIRLEY HIGH STREET 0847 654312

....

HOW DID WE DO?

....

see rule about aphrodisiacs

2 SCOTCH EGGS	£1.49
BLACK SAMBUCA (750ML)	£12.99
BUMPER PK ROUGH RIDERS CONDOMS	£3.65
BANANAS (6 PACK)	£1.09
FRESH WHIPPING CREAM (250ML)	£1.99
HOT CHILLI SAUCE	£1.35
KY JELLY	£2.99
BABY OIL	£2.10
PEDIGREE CHUM	£3.00
CUCUMBER	£0.79

enough said

for the rescue dog you've rescued at home

food for thought

TOTAL	£31.44
CASH	£40.00
CHANGE DUE	£8.66

SIGN UP FOR CLUBCARD

You could have earned 51 Clubcard points in this transaction

....

19/06/11 11.18 3238 072 9072 7676

#16 IF YOU CAN'T PULL AT A WEDDING, THERE'S SOMET WRONG WITH YOU

If all else fails, weddings are good places to pull both for fellas and birds. Everyone is happy, feeling romantic and most people think how lovely it would be if they too were one day to be getting married. Don't rush it though. Wait till the night do when everyone's pissed and look for the girls who are sitting round the edge during the slow dances and pounce.

If you can't pull a single person at a wedding then there's somet wrong with you. If that does happen read this book again or carry it around in your pocket for reference.

GOOD SONGS TO REQUEST AT WEDDINGS TO GET GIRLS ON'T DANCE FLOOR:

'Get Off' by Prince — It's got some sexy lyrics in that song.

'Lets Talk About Sex' by Salt and Pepper — again sexy but fun.

Or you could go romantic and ask for a bit of Dirty Dancing Time of me Life. Girls love that. And thanks to doing Lets Dance for Comic Relief with me mate Paddy (we didn't win we came second, robbed we were) I know all the dance moves to that song.

I pulled Emma Willis from telly at a wedding years ago and let me tell ya she could lift me up just as well as Paddy did. She has the most beautiful eyes. She's a lovely lass. At the end of the night I went back to the hotel and smashed her to bits.

We're just good friends now like but sometimes I can still see that sparkle in her eyes, sending me that message that she wants me to re-introduce the 'tash' to 'gash'! Ooooosh! Emma if you're reading this, you've got me number.

OOOOOSH!

ONLINE

If you've got a computer thingy, why not do a bit of window shopping online? Online dating used to be for lonely virgins that cun't meet birds or fellas in real life. But now it's the done thing. I've never done it cos I can pull birds just whilst I'm getting me Sunday Sport on a morning, but the principles stay the same.

snatch.com

GET YER END AWAY

#17 ALWAYS EXAGGERATE YOUR WEALTH

Always lie and say you've got a flash car and a big house. Scientists in NASA have proven that women prefer men with dollors rather than looks. Lucky for me I've got both. I'm not saying that they're money grabbing so and so's, its just that they are attracted to men that can look after them.

How do you fink Mick Hucknall from Simply Ginger pulled? He's not a looker is he...he's' got plenty of wedge though. Can't believe he's been out with Martin McCutcheon. Apparently she sicked up in his ginger dreadlocks. By I bet he was pissed off. Fink she's engaged now so I'm gonna stop going on about her. Waste of time. I totally misread the signals there I thought I was in. Enough. Enough Martin bleeding McCutcheon.

WHATEVER

I don't need the sunnies of course — this is just to show ugly people how to wear them with style

#18

, If You've got a face like a pig use a picture of someone that's attractive. Or wear large sunglasses, simple as that.

#19 ALWAYS SAY YOU LOVE ANIMALS
(BUT NOT SO MUCH THAT YOU WANNA MAKE LOVE TO THEM)

The ladies love it if they fink you go all soft over an animal – it makes them fink you'll be a good parent. Weird but true. But some animal people take it a bit far and it gets a bit weird. My mate once made love to his dog with a pencil. It was the wrongest thing I've ever seen. They're still together though and happily married. That's a true story apart from the marriage.

I wish I had a belly button but dogs don't have belly buttons do they?

OOOOOSH!

#20 GLAMOURIZE YOUR LIFE STYLE

You don't wanna look like a boring fart. Nobody online tells the truth. If they say they do they're lying. Talk about all your hobbies: extreme sports and stuff. Snowboarding, wake boarding, surfboarding etc. (which stands for Et Cetera which means 'and other things').

Just before my title fight

At the wakeboard world championsh

Cattle rustling in Texas

Minge diving backstage

OOOOOSH!

Trucking around

Just bought this chopper

Tamsin from telly asking if she can blow me. BANG!

Me in me back garden

OOOOOSH!

BANTER

Where as men only care about a woman's bits and bobs, women apparently are more bothered about a bloke's personality. This chapter is all about having one (or pretending you have one) via the power of banter.

Banter can create the illusion that you have a personality even if you've got nowt. You will learn the importance of verbal talking chat and conversing. You will become a linguistic wizard and will gain the power to access a woman's magic door.
Either the front or the back!

#21 NEVER BE COCKY, ALWAYS BE CHEEKY

To get your banter spot on, you need to be the right side of cocky. 'Pint of lager and your phone number please.' Said that once to a bar maid and she even threw in a packet of cheese and onion crisps. And the rest.

#22 BREAK THE ICE WITH A CHAT UP LINE

So once you've identified your target, a chat up line is an easy way to break the ice.

Try one of these:

- Do you eat frosties because you're bringing out the tiger in me. You look grrrrrrrrreat! I'd love to have it off with ya.

- I know milk does a body good, but DAMN... How much have you been drinking? I'd love to see you gargle it.

- I hope you know CPR cause you take my breath away. You can give me t' kiss of life if you want and put ya tongue in.

You're gonna get yourself arrested you. It's gotta be illegal to look that good. Super bang. I'd let you stick yer finger up me arse.

If I had the chance to rearrange the alphabet, I would put U and I together and sex you up till it hurt me.

I'm glad I've got a sat nav on me iphone 4, cos I keep getting lost in your eyes. But its hard to keep looking at them cos you've got equally beautiful tits.

Are you tired? Because you've been running through my mind all night. Would you like to toss me?

Lucky for me I don't need chat up lines. Cos I'm a minge magnet ladies normally throw themselves at me. Not sure if that's just cos I'm on't telly or cos I am actually just physically attractive. Either way I'm not bothered.

OOSH!

#23 ALWAYS BACK UP YOUR BANTER

But remember, you can't really give it all that 'Is your dad a thief, cos he's stolen all the stars in't sky and put them in your eye balls', if you can't back it up with loads of good banter afterwards. Ask the girl as many questions about them so you sound interested in the mind and not just their bangers. If you're stuck for questions, here's some questions that start off great topics of conversation...

You ever been to Japan?

I love yer shoes, what are they la boutins?

Can you body POP?

Did you know that when one of their teeth falls out another one roles up in its place?

Do you like sharks?

How old is your mum?

Banter
Do you like crisps?
Did you see the remake of 'Fame'? Ya know in't song 'Fame' when she sings 'Fame, remember my name' what is her name? She never says does she. What do you think her name is?
Has anyone ever told ya you look like Lucy Pinder?
Did you go to an all girls school? What was that like, was it nice?
OOOOOSH!
What is the first record you bought?
What's the worst thing you're ever done? Whats the best thing? (Quickly follow that up with 'Mine was coming here tonight to meet you.' Ooooooosh!)
I like your hair, whats that called, a perm?

#24
DON'T BE AFRAID TO USE PROPS

fig 1.

BIG KAHUNA

So you've got your chat down, with that you'll need some good props to back up your bullshit. For i.e (not sure what i.e. stands for but I've seen it somewhere) in my kitchen I have a surfboard lent against the wall. It obviously suggests that I've just come back from a surfing trip and haven't yet had time to put it away. Where did I go surfing? In Australia! With my mate Jason Donavon. How do I know Jason Donovan? Well I have my own Charity called Lemon-aid and I went down to Heart FM where old Jason Donovan has a show and asked him if he'd get involved by doing a sponsored bath in some beans. He said yes cos celebrities love doing charity stuff cos it makes them look good, and we hit it off just like that.

Or another idea: some flowers and card from your mum saying thanks for being the best son in the world. Girls love that shit. Shows your softer side.

R.I.P GARY

A dog bowl is good too. You can pretend that ya pet dog has just died. She'll feel sorry for you and you'll probably get a hand job almost instantly. Especially if you lay the tears on. Look vunerable but not weak. She'll be tossing you off before you can say potato! Emu style!

#25
CREATE A BIT OF INTRIGUE

As well as props laid about the house or flat or whatever you live in, maybe a cave, there are some props you can wear. Do you know how many back doors I've smashed in simply from just one little ice-breaking question such as 'What have you done to your hand?'

Opened many a back door...

Highly unlikely

But remember, be creative with your porky's but don't mention unicorns or Prince as not many people have met a unicorn or Prince so its highly unlikely that they actually exist.

OOOOOSH!

Here are some ideas for the lads:

1. A framed map of the world or planet. Shows you're interested in travel and a book/art book/something shit like that so she thinks you're cultured.

2. Some running shoes. Tell her you're training for the London Marathon to raise money for divvys and so displaying the caring side of your personality.

3. The size of your telly is very important. It projects your wealth. Never go smaller than a 60" plazma, no matter how small your living room is.

4. Some theatre tickets. Although it's boring, girls love the theatre. I took a girl to see Disney on Ice Skates. The way she gobbled her hotdog down in front of me spoke a thousand words. Her back doors were history!

through the back doors!

...And here are some for the ladies

1. Fill your fridge with those ready meals that you just put in t' microwave. If you go out of the room that's the first thing a man will do, look in yer fridge. Get a few cans in there too.

2. A pile of ironing is always a good idea. Having a bird who is willing to do your ironing is the cherry on the cake. And have a bra on top of the pile, and some knickers. There's no way he'll be able to resist a quick sniff if you're not looking. It's like putting cheese in front of a mouse.

3. An X-Box or Playstation is a must. It completes the look of underneath ya telly. Any telly without an X-Box or Playstation underneath it looks too bare, looks daft. You gotta send out the vibe that you're one of the lads but with bangers!

4. A shelve full of DVDs. You can tell a lot by a girl by what films she's into. Have something naughty in there too. He'll fink he's struck gold if he thinks you like watching porn.

5. A potters wheel. Later on if all goes well you could be recreating that scene from 'Ghost'.

Clean and fresh like.

O O O O O SH!

#26 DROP SUBLIMINAL CLUES

Another good thing to do is to drop subliminal clues into conversation. You ave to be quite clever to do this but here's an example to explain what I mean. 'Can I just say you look beautiful. Give me a second to attract the waiters attention. Your hair looks amazing! What is that like a blow dry job? Later, sorry I mean waiter can we have some wine please?'

Derren Brown — master
of the subliminal message

Now to the untrained eye you might not be able to see the subliminal message, but here it is again with the subliminals in red.

CAN I just say **YOU** look
beautiful **GIVE ME** a second
to attract the waiters attention.
Your hair looks amazing!
What is that like **A BLOW**
dry **JOB** ?
LATER sorry I mean waiter
can we have some wine please?

These words will float into her brain and help her decide the outcome. It's her notion, you've just helped put it there. It's like the Matrix sort of thing.

OTHER SUBLIMINAL MESSAGES

I think it's really important to give a bit back. I'M a supporter of a charity that helps HUNGry children in Africa. It doesn't just give them food though, they get skills and tools for life LIKE A HORSE.

I CANT take my eyes off you. STOP laughing at my jokes – I'll get a big head. I keep THINKING it's ABOUT time I found someone as SMASHING as you. YOUR front and BACK are equally gorgeous. Oh mind the DOORS on your way IN.

0
0
0
0
0
5
H
!

#27 PERFECT THE PLAYGROUND FLIRT

This goes back to school days when you were too young to understand ya emotions. We aven't a clue what to do. I remember climbing the ropes in games and P.E. lessons and as I got to the top I'd feel like I was gonna waz in me pants, obviously I was having a cheap frill. Back then the method of flirtation with the girls was basically taking the piss out of them and before you knew it, you'd scored. This way of flirting is still commonly used in adulthood. Take for instance on 'Celebrity Juice' when I give Fearne lots of grief about her nostrils – it's cos I proper fancy her and try to belittle her so I can control my emotions towards her (and if you see her in the street don't tell her any of this, just moon at her). I have a lot of respect for that woman. I don't wanna get seriers with her or owt, I just wanna have a go on her. I bet she's proper mad in't sack. Nice girl next door image but in the sack a proper dirt bag.

I'll show yer what I mean with a few case studies:

1. STACEY SOLOMAN

Me: 'Now then Stace, I've gotta be honest with ya. If you were in Wind in the Willows, those weasels would be all over you like a rash, you sexy rodent!'

See, this is a left field comment. It sounds like abuse but I'm actually telling her she's fit. And she is, she's got amazing legs and top draw bangers.

If you're reading this Stacey, call me. You've got me number

Sexy rodent

OOOOOSH!

Gypsy campsite

2. CHRISTINA RICCI

Me: 'How do Christina. Look at the size of your forehead! You wanna be careful gypsy's don't pull up on there. I bet a fringe would look lovely on you.'

Again, the old piss-take is cleverly softened with a compliment see.

3. JESSICA SIMPSON

Me: 'Hey up Jessica! By you're looking well. Yer carrying a bit of timber aren't yer! You look good for it though.'

Everyone know that the phrase 'looking well' means you've put a bit of timber on. It's a reverse compliment and still comes under playground flirting in the adult realm.

Looking well

#28 MASTER THE ELBOW GROPE

Squeeze here for fresh lemon juice

elbow boob rub

OOOOOOSH!

Sometimes straight to the point flirting is all that is required – like coming out of the toilet with yer wanger still out and pretending you didn't know it was out or getting a elbow grope of their bangers. That's a classic and they love it. I don't know what it is about a cheeky elbow grope... it's sneaky but obvious at the same time.

Simply stand in front of a girl and gently brush your elbow on their breast as if by accident. They never complain.

#29 EVERY MAN SHOULD HAVE TOP 5 PRIMARY SKILLS

This is something you should have prepared in your mind for when a girl asks you 'what are your top 5 main primary skills?' If you don't have any then develop some. Here's mine

1. Having if off

2. Dancing – all kinds from break dancing to Russian Cossack dancing

3. Drawing on't ipad and with felt tips and stuff

4. Snowboarding

5. Skateboarding

I have 6 actually. I can do the sound of a Victorian bicycle but this can't be demonstrated in print.

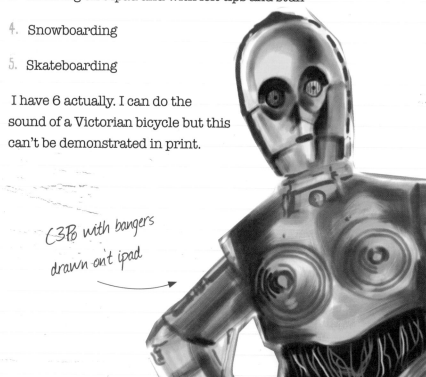

C3P0 with bangers drawn on't ipad

PRMARY SKILLS FOR WOMEN

And girls, it's worth having a few skills of your own. If you can't do anything, why not try some of these:

1. Knitting

2. Pole dancing

3. Lap dancing

4. Cooking right good food

5. Ironing to a professional level of expertise

Laura Whitmore from MTV is a right tidy pole dancer, especially when it's my pole!

Love you Gran xxx

#30 BE LIKE A LOCKET
– HARD ONT OUTSIDE, SOFTER AND JUICY ONT INSIDE.

Women like a man to be strong but soft and caring. Sounds like mixed messages don't it. That's women for yer. You have to project that macho façade but still show your gentle side, like caring about brocken animals. Try and get in touch with your feminine side. If like me you find that hard cos you are all man and don't have a feminine side, then you have to create one (creating and pretending are basically the same fing).

Try the following to project your softer side:

1. Watch these films – Titanic, Dirty Dancing, Beaches, Serendipity, The Notebook, Bridget Jones's'ssss Diary, Pretty Woman, Ghost and of course Marley and Me.

2. Visit a dog rescue type place fing. Or just lie and say you do. Remember girls love animals and so do you. They pecifically like horses, so express an interest in them even though they are horrible and too big for humans to ride.

WARNING! consecutive viewing of these films could give you too much of a soft side and you could end up wanting to smoke sausage. Don't do all these films in one session. Just one a week should do the trick.

3. Help old people over the road.

Here Owen Wilson is with Jennifer Aniston. Super bang! In 'Marley & Me' he shows his softer side by pretending he likes guide dogs. Women love a man that likes guide dogs it show's you have a heart.

O
O
O
O
O
S
H
!

4. Buy flowers for your kitchen. I don't know why but women like that – flowers in't kitchen.

5. Eat special K for breakfast.

6. When you see something beautiful, a nice view from a hospital bed whilst visiting a sick child, a painting, a wedding dress in a shop window, try your hardest to push out a tear. This will show you have emotion. If you can cry at the sight of beauty then that is deep shit!

Banter Glossary

COMPLIMENTS:

You're tidy you: You are pretty

You are bang!: You are very attractive

You're bang tidy you are!: You are enormously sexually attractive

You're F.A.F you are: You are as gorgeous as sex itself

Bangtastic: Sexy / Amazing / Sexually amazing

I'd smash her back doors in, I would: I'd go to any lengths to seduce that lady / My desire for her is unrestrainable

I would destroy her: I can't repress what I feel for her / She is an outrageous looker

Does your cookie want some cream?: Ultra-flirtatious proposition

Fancy going twos on a bastard?: Would you like to copulate? / Shall we have passionate unprotected sex?

Let the tash see the gash: I'm growing tired of looking at your clothes

I'd go through you like a train: I'm a vigorous lover / I wouldn't need a second invitation / I wouldn't need an invitation

As fit as a butcher's dog: Sexually attractive

I'm riding a lady wave: I'm single most days, taken every night / Beautiful women are scrambling for me

LESS COMPLIMENTARY REMARKS

You're fick as well: Your stupid as well as unattractive

Wankor (n): American for wanker / someone who finds comfort in their hand / A person so irritating it must be deliberate

Tossor (n): American for tosser / A boundless idiot

By it were shit: I'm gravely disappointed

Get a bag on your head, you moose: Cover your face, you hideous beast / You appeal only from the neck down

Are you speaking Punjabi?: I can't understand you, are you speaking something other than English?

By you're fat: My goodness, you are plump / Reveal less of yourself

Dingbat (n): An ignorant fool

MISCELLANEOUS

Lesbican (n): A female homosexual / A female homosexual member of the Republican Party

Bean flicker (n): A female homosexual

Sausage smoker / Hormone sexual (n): A homosexual man

Yu-Ya (n): Female privates

Bangers (n): Breasts

Milk Trucks (n): Breasts

Cadbury's Cream Eggs (n): Breasts

Boy tits (n): Small breasts

Fit Potato (n): A minxy girl / A stunner

Potaaatoooo (n): Potato

Love tussle (n): Romantic entanglement

Lezz off (v): Dabble in lesbianism

Trump (v): Breaking wind

Pecifically (adv): Specifically

TLC (n): Tender Lemon Cuddles

Yaroosky! (excl): Joy!

Sphincter (n): A mythical Egyptian creature

Minge magnet (n): A sexually attractive man / A smooth talker

Minge master (n): An enormously sexually attractive man / A ladykiller

OOOOO SH!

ONE NIGHTSTANDS

It's very common if you're a man to be called a stud if you have a lot of one nightstands. On the other hand if you're a woman having one nightstands, many will regard you as a dirty slapper. But I love dirty slappers! They're so much fun and easy going, and as time goes on I'm sure that the stigma of the dirty slapper is fastly eradicating. So here's some simple rules for having a one nightstand. Enjoy yerself!

One night stands

#31 CREATE A PET NAME FOR YOUR ONE NIGHT STAND

You don't want to get too personal with them whilst having it off or it could lead to a relationship and that's defeating the whole idea of it. So there's no point learning her name, you're not gonna marry her or owt. Here are some ideas for pet names:

Baby

Cheeky baby

Darling

Petal

Sweet Cheeks

Butter tits

#32

Always leave on your socks and shoes so you can make a fast getaway if need be.

Enough said.

OOOOSH!

#33 DON'T SLEEP THERE

As soon as you've done the deed, clean it up and get outta there. Otherwise it could lead to another date, like breakfast or lunch (lunch? I'm catching London. I mean dinner. This is the eating pattern - breakfast , dinner, tea, supper). Anyway, you get the idea: get the job done and go.

#34 BE AS DIRTY AS YOU WANT

It's animal magnetism that's brought you together so act like an animal. Don't do a shit in the corner of the room, but you know what I mean. Get it all out of your system, you're not gonna see them again so don't by shy. If you've ever fancied going up trap two then try it.

Let your inner animal come out.
They've got the right idea.

#35 NEVER LET THE ACTION TAKE PLACE AT YOUR GAFF

If the deed is done at your place, you can't take your leave when you want to, so always try and go back to hers. Similarly, if they ask for your number give them the number of a friend you no longer speak to. you may need it in the future but its got to be on your terms.

OOOOOSH!

FIRST DATES

Get yer snakeskin shoes, you've pulled. Now what?
You've got to go on a first date. There's all different kinds
of first dates. There's the first date after you've already
shagged at the back of a club. There's the first date
after you've stalked them online. There's the first date
where you might not remember their name. There's the
first date where you might not remember what they
look like. And then there's the first date that's
the worst date: You don't remember their name,
or what they look like and he/she turns up and is a
moose! Whichever it is, here are a few ideas to keep
you both amused.

#36 TREAT HER TO A HORROR FILM

A classic first date is a trip to the cinema. A horror film is particularly good. When she gets scared and wants you to protect her from the boogie man, you can slip your arm round her and play the gent.

I'd give this film 5 stars

the lemon saga
new lemon

Then offer her some of your popcorn which your have previously secretly put your tallywacker in. Make a hole in't bottom of t' box. When she dips her hand in the box to take thus said popcorn she'll grab a right handful! Hopefully she'll not freak out and bash you off emu style instead!

Obviously your popcorn will de destroyed after this so make sure you've sneaked another bag in from home. Yer can't watch a film without popcorn.

0
0
0
0
0
5
H
!

TIP: Start licking her ears. Not like you're licking a lolly, but like you are softly making love to her ear with your tongue. All soft and gentle like. Within no time she'll be all over yer...

#37 SPLASH OUT ON A SPREE

If you're a man, shopping don't sound fun does it. But ladies love shopping as it releases the same chemical to the brain as it does when they're having their breasts fondled. Again, it's science. And for you, it's a good way to have a look at her body, she's proper letting you stare at it! Whatever you do, when she's trying dresses on and asking you what you think, whatever you do, bullshit! It's not a bad bullshit, it's a good bullshit. Tell her she looks great in anything she comes out in. Tell her she'd look great in a sack full of horse shit.

What women think about

- meeting me
- snogging me
- having their breasts fondled by me
- getting their back doors smashed in by me
- shopping

Plus, most of the shops she's gonna wanna go into are gonna be filled with bang tidy birds and maybe some of those birds are gonna be more bang tidier than the bird you're with. If you see something else you like then don't feel bad if you wanna get their number, you're under no special contract, yer just out shopping. You'll soon know if you wanna go on a second date with her or not. So fellas shopping is a good thing. Simple as peas.

O
O
O
O
O
S
H
!

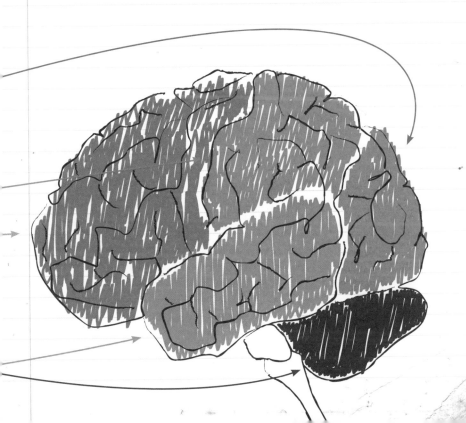

#38 TREAT HER TO AN OLD-FASHIONED DINNER DATE

A dinner date is pretty standard. That's the norm, but there's no browny points for originality. If you do go for dinner make sure you order for her. Order her something shaped like yer manhood that way she can be suggestive towards you by the way she eats it.

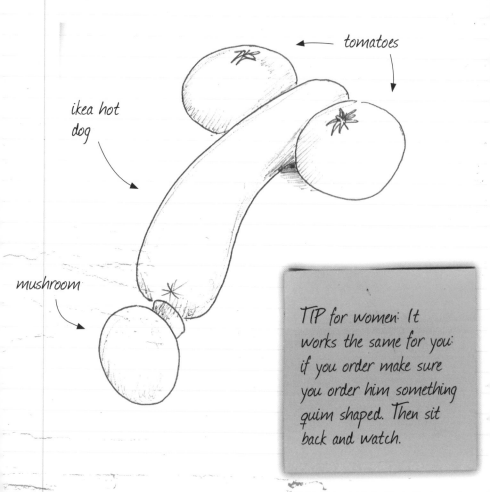

tomatoes

ikea hot dog

mushroom

TIP for women: It works the same for you: if you order make sure you order him something quim shaped. Then sit back and watch.

#39 SPLASH ABOUT IN THE BATHS

A first date that I'm particularly fond of that not many people seem to think of is the swimming baths. Not only is it a great way to keep fit you can see if she is fit! Take some goggles, have a right good look at each other.

Show off by demonstrating your diving ability. If you've passed your bronze swimming award, bring a pair of pyjamas and a rubber brick and retrieve the brick whilst wearing your pyjamas. I don't know why they do that... I think it's to replicate saving somebody. But as if you're gonna have your pyjamas on whilst you see somebody drowning, and why do you have to be wearing pyjamas to save somebody? Anywhere, she'll be impressed.

O
O
O
O
O
S
H
!

I usually swim naked not in pyjamas!

#40 PUSH OUT A TEAR

Once you're back at the love shack, make sure you've got some romantic tune playing in't back ground. Maybe Terrens Trent D'arby 'Sign ya name across me heart.' If you've got any acting skills try push a tear out. Tell her that her beauty reduces you to tears and you can totally imagine falling deeply in love with her. But you don't wanna rush it. You wanna take it step at a time so you can cherish each tender moment with her. If you're American, that's 'TendOR'. Trust me, she'll love it.

TIP: Keep a glass of chopped onions down the back of your sofa and the tears'll come easierly. She'll love it.

#41 CLEAN THE WINDOWS AND FEED THE HORSE

Depending on the chemistry or respect you have for them should dictate how far you should go on a first date. To be respectful of the lady I think its best to do the gentlemanly thing and go no further than cleaning the windows and feeding the horse, all over the top of the clothes. Don't go in the pants yet and stay over the bra.

0
0
0
0
0
5
H
!

#42 ENJOY THE SILENCES

I fink the reason so many women like me is that I'm never stuck for anything to say, but now and again its nice to have those quiet moments. Those awkward silences that when you're so comfortable with someone it actually doesn't feel awkward. Of course women love these moments. So if you've never had one, orchestrate one. It will feel awkward but she'll like that fact you're having one and have told her it doesn't feel awkward. Go with it and you'll be cupping boobs faster than a high speed boob cupping machine.

#43 LEARN HOW TO HOLD A CONVERSATION

Girls like to talk. Talk, talk, talk. When lads meet up we laugh and drink and can't remember what anyone said. To talk to a woman you gotta have more than that. Educate them with things you know. If you don't know anything or yer fick then watch the History Channel and the Biography Channel. It's also a good idea to know what women like to chat about. You'll need to be able to talk about the following:

Charlotte Church

No longer going out with that rugby player. And she has lost some timber. She is all grown up and bang!

Kerry Katona from the jungle

Kerry used to work for Iceland selling chicken dinosaurs for one pound (and mini pizzas and prawn rings, all for one pound!). She no longer goes out with Brian from Westlife (one of the best boy bands in't world). She also no longer goes out with that plumber, was he a plumber? Sure I bought a pirate copy of 'Jurrasic Park' from him on Leeds market once. Think he was called Mark. She's now got her life back on track, new hair and a 3 million pound house. Think she's sold it now though.She can bunk up with me if she likes.

The difference between Chantelle and Chanelle

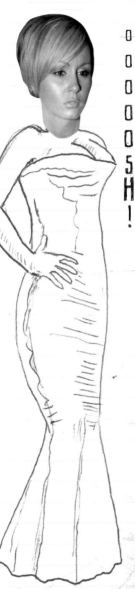

Chantelle is bang tidy and went out with a man called Preston who dressed like he was from the past. Then she went out with another man, then another.

Chanelle is bang tidy and was a Victoria Beckham look-a-like but more council estate than posh, still F.A.F though. She went out with someone called Ziggy in Big Brother, then went out with another man, and another. She now gets her jacksy out in lads mag and so she should, I would destroy her! Oh she's now also had a baby which makes her more relatable to other women.

OOOOOSH!

Spot the difference

GMTV

Now called 'Daybreak' and is hosted by a man and Christine fit potato Bleakly!

La Bootins

Ladies shoes with red soles. They cost more than a cheap car so be aware of girls that like these.

Jimmy

A well known designer shoe as worn by nipple chin. A good idea is to learn as many designer shoe names as you can just so you can look at a girls shoe and say 'They're beautiful, what are they Jimmy shoes?'

TOWIE

A documentary called The Only Way Is Essex. It's got loads of fit birds in it, a tubby lad and a hunk. It's a bit like Hollyoacks but REAL!

Dirty Dancing

'I ate a water melon'. This is the line from the film Dirty Dancing. Birds love it and will repeat it a lot. If she wants to spend a night in watching this film with ya, do not expect owt too dirty despite the title. There's not even any tits in it.

fit potato

#44 DON'T DATE A CO-WORKER

It is a golden rule... but what if she's as fit as a butchers dog? Just treat her as a friend with benefits. If you do end up romancing her always make sure booze is involved. Then you can write it off the next day saying you can't even remember the night before. You don't know what she's talking about. She's probably just been fantasising about you and made it up. Daft bird.

my fuck buddies

Properly dating a co-worker though is asking for trouble... with you every minute of the day, what a nightmare. That's why me and Fearne Cotton don't date. It'd spoil our beautiful working relationship.

O
O
O
O
O
S
H
!

If you're reading this Fearne we're just fuck buddies OK?

> HELLO I CAN'T MAKE IT TONIGHT I'VE FALLEN IN THE BATH.

#45 IF YOU CANCEL A DATE, ALWAYS HAVE A GOOD EXCUSE

We've all done it. We've arranged a date but decided not to go through with it at a later date but you need to let them down gently. It's only fair. Here's some good excuses for not turning up that should protect her dignity.

> I FORGOT TO TELL YOU: I'M HORMONE SEXUAL. I THOUGHT I WAS STRAIGHT BUT I'M NOT I JUST LOVE SMOKING WILLYS.

> YOU NOT GONNA BELIEVE IT BUT I WENT FOR A WALK ON THE MOORS AND I GOT BITTEN BY A WEREWOLF. I DON'T THINK I'M SAFE TO BE AROUND.

SEX

This is what we've been working so hard for. The banter, the clobber, the compliments, it all comes down to this. Only beer and Sunday dinner comes close to the act that we all live for: sex. Being a Northern sex god what I don't know about sex in't worth knowing. I am very good at it and if you've been paying attention you too will be at it quicker than you can say Shaaaaa-ting!

#46 PUT ON A DvD TO GET YOU IN T' MOOD

(1) 'Basic Instinct' staring Sharon Stone and Michael Douglas makes you wanna screw like a rabbit. It even made me wanna shove me fingers in my birds mouth just like Michael does to Sharon for some reason. If you decide to do this make sure you've washed your hands previously. Must be horrible for the girl if the man has been playing with his keys or spare change in his pocket. Metal fingers.

(2) 'Wild Things' starring Neve Campbell and Denise Richards has an explicit ménage a trios scene involving the girls and the high school guidance counsellor played by Matt Dillon. See the un-rated version on DVD. You'll want your missus to get her mate round and recreate the same scene. Denise Richards is so fit is this film she should be told off.

(3) 'Three' staring Kelly Brook. Plenty of scenes in this film to get you in the mood. Kelly Brook is so fit it sometimes cancels her self out. You forget how fit she is cos she's soooo fit. Imagine being stranded on island with her... Well, if you watch this film you can imagine that your missus is her and you're stranded on an island with her. F.A.F.

(4) '9 and a ½ Weeks' starring Kim Basinger and Mickey Rouke. This film is well known for its well known erotic sadomasochistic scene (not sure what that means). All I can say is food is used and it's as hot as hell. Not the food but the way the food is used. Food can be very sexy especially when its being eaten off a hot bod like Kim Basinger's. This film has no doubt been recreated in many a kitchen. I've done it myself. All I had in the fridge at the time was some brown source and some scotch eggs. You know how to use your imagination!

5) 'Cruel Intentions' is saucy as hell. Starring a nest of bang tidy birds: Rees Witherspoon, Salma Blair and Sarah Michelle Geller, (that's Buffy from Buffy t' Vampire Slayer). I mean who wouldn't want to buff her? In this film you get to see her snog Salma. So romantic. Lovely.

OOOOOSH!

F.A.F – my desert island dish

#47 LEARN HOW TO TURN A WOMAN ON

What is it that's gonna really get her going? Let me share a few tips with ya.

Firstly, take it nice and slow. Whisper sweet nothings in her ear, right breathy like 'You make me wobbly like a jelly, oooosh'

Or 'Would you like me to kiss your boobies on't end, right on't end. Not near the end, but right on't bloody end!'

Or 'I'm as stiff as a brick for ya. I wanna sex you off, on top, underneath, all over yer god damn sexy body.'

Or 'I'm gonna lick you out like a cream egg' (They love that).

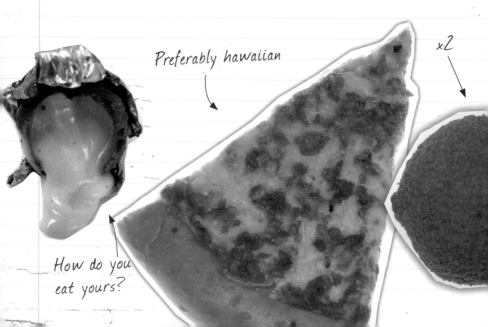

Preferably hawaiian

x2

How do you eat yours?

#48 TRY AN APHRODISIAC

So you've got the DVD on but you'll need some snacks to enhance the effects. Try some of these aphrodisiacs that will 100% guarantee you getting her or him in't mood

Pizza + 4 bottles of wine

A couple of scotch eggs + 5 shots of zambooka

A plate of hot dogs + 6 bottles of wine

Any food shaped like a tally is good

Plenty of this is a good loosener. My favourite is Bianco

OOOOOSH!

#49 PICK YOUR VENUE CAREFULLY

Don't have sex near a police station. Coppers don't like it. One of my mates Daft Terry gone down just for having a piss outside once. Also worth avoiding having it off outside schools too (unless you go to that school) might look a bit odd.

#50 KEEP IT SPICY

Nothing worse than doing it in the same position hour after hour. Keep it spicy. Here's a few of my favourites to keep the spark alive.

1. In't bath is good but you'll have to get out straight away otherwise you'll have the jizz monster after you.

2. If she's not much of a looker, have her sat on top facing the other way then you can imagine its some one else, anyone from Lorraine Kelly to Jenny Folkner depending on your taste.

I love a bit of LK first thing in't morning

3. One of those sex swings. Although I've never done it, me mate Mick has and he said it's the bollox!

4 Doggy style is nice. Plus you can also play with yer Nintendo at the same time. Just lay it on her back.

Got my highest score on Donkey Kong playing it like this

5. In't park against a tree from behind. Be aware of squirrels, it can put you off having one staring at you.

OOOOOO5H!

Peru ⟶

#51 CHOKE THE CHICKEN AS OFTEN AS YOU NEED TO

There's many different terms for giving yourself a bit of passion and that's because everyone does it. There's nowt wrong with it and you should do it as often as you like. But this in't an act just to be done by yerself.

If for some insane reason I've gone a day without sex I often pump fist. Don't feel odd if you have to have a go more than once a day.

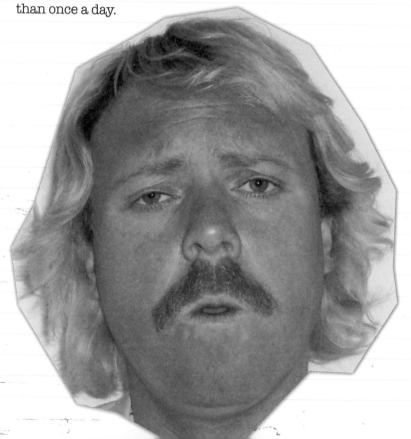

OOOOOOSH!

HAND SHANDY

BASH THE BISHOP

WANK

JERK OFF *(if you're American)*

BEAT ONE OFF

CRANK THE SHANK

HAVE A SHERMAN TANK

KNOCK ONE OUT

FLICK THE BEAN

DATE WITH MADAME PALM

TOSS

TEASE ONE OUT

SPANK THE MONKEY

NUMBER FOUR

TOMMY TANK

LAMB SHANK

WRIST WORKOUT

BLIND MAN'S VICE

KNUCKLE SHUFFLE

EMPTY THE CHAMBER

TAME THE TIGER

PUMP THE FIST

MILK THE MONSTER

INSIDER TRADE

CHOKE THE CHICKEN

WALK THE PLANK

TACTICAL

TUG

WARNING!
Be very careful bashing the bishop using shower gel if it goes down the external urethral orifice or wee hole it can sting like no other sting you've ever had!

#52 IF YER EVER AWAY FROM YER PARTNER, HAVE SOME SEXY PHONE SEX

But if you're one of those people that has, good for you. I hope it didn't hurt. Of course there is other ways to have phone sex and that's to phone someone and tell them some sexy things down't phone. This preferably should be with someone you're in a relationship with, otherwise its just a dirty phonecall and you can get in trouble for this;

If you don't know where to start, here's a bit of inspiration:
Alright love. I've got it in my hand and I'm stroking it thinking it's you. I'm imagining I'm kissing yer bangers and feeling them both clockwise and anti-clockwise.

ARRRRRRH THAT'S IT I'VE SPILLED ME BEANS.

I LOVE YOU.

#53

ALWAYS USE PROTECTION ON YOUR ERECTION, OR YOU MIGHT GET AN INFECTION!

Listen to your uncle
Keith, he knows best.

RELATIONSHIPS

If you've got yerself into a spot of bother and some bird is starting to call you her boyfriend, my advice is to set the record straight – quick. Else, before you know it she'll be wanting you to call her every night. But sometimes it can be worth it. Here are some rules to make sure things don't get out of hand.

#54 TREAT 'EM MEAN AND KEEP 'EM KEEN

That don't necessarily mean be an utter bastard, it just means don't be a kiss arse. No one respects a kiss arse. So you shouldn't come over too needy if you're going for the whole relationship fing. Don't be there for them when they click their fingers. Be un-obtainable. Don't always pick up the phone. Whilst with them be respectable but make out you've got other fings going on. Pick up calls from other girls whilst yer with her even if you're not getting calls from other girls. Here's some fake conversations you can memorise if you're not good at making up.

'HELLO PETAL'

[pause while imaginary fit bird speaks]

'HOW'S TRICKS?'

#55 NEVER GET CAUGHT EYEING UP ANOTHER GIRL

If you're with your 'girl friend' but are surround by other tidy birds, there's nowt wrong with having a look. It's only window shopping. But of course she'll go off her box and be vexed to the max if she catches ya so you need to know how to eye up the birds on the sneak.

First up, the law. Never go to the beach without dark sunglasses. Why do you think they were invented? To look at birds without your bird knowing you're looking at other birds, or indeed other birds knowing you are looking at them whilst your bird doesn't know you're looking at them. Don't be blatant with it. Look away from the bird you are looking at but avert your eyes towards your target.

Or pretend you have hay fever. Sneeze into a tissue, but rip a small hole into the tissue and peak through that. Simple.

Essential perv wear

Recently found out that this woman is a man. To clarify I did not bang her/him

OOOOSH!

#56 MEET HER MATES - IF SHE'S TIDY, THEY PROBABLY ARE TOO

It might seem pretty pointless meeting her mates but it's a good indication of what someone's really like, and you never know they might have some fit mates. Maybe fitter than her or him.

Having a bird with lots of fit mates is good as it makes you look like a stud. Usually tidy people hang out with other tidy people. So, if you're in a group of tidy people, it's highly likely that you meet lots of other tidy people! Again, more science.

#57 AVOID MEETING THE PARENTS FOR AT LEAST TWO WEEKS

You should stay away from this act as long as you can. What interest have you get in their parents? Why do you need this hassle? You only meet the parents when you've been seeing him or her for a long time, when its getting really seriers. Maybe after the second week. If you've lasted two weeks with the same person then there's obviously something special there - weather it's a bangtastic arse or a lovely pair of jebs.

Here's how you should greet a parent of someone you are smashing and get round the tricky questions. In this scenario I'll play me meeting a parent.

'Narcolepsy is a terrible affliction, sir. Thank flip I was there to hold Sheridan up.'

DOOOSH!

Hello sir my name is Keith, let me tell you who I am if you don't know who I am. My name is Keith. I run my own business called Securipole and I am a TV host on the telly.

So you're the prat off the telly she's been seeing.

Yes sir I have nothing but respect for her and might I say you have a lovely garden.

Didn't I see you in't paper with your tongue down Sheridan Smith's throat?

Yes that was me but my tongue was firmly stuck in my own throat. Unfortunately Sheridan suffers from narcolepsy. I was holding her up whilst my friend had just told a very humourous joke.

You have a wonderful house sir.

You're arse kiss. I can see right through you. I know your sort.

I have eyes only for your daughter. Please take these two tickets for Celebrity Juice and Holly and Fearne's phone numbers.

[Parent is now on the phone heavy breath to either Holly or Fearne.]

I have won

#58 KEEP CALM AND WIN THE MINGE!

No matter what grief the parents give you, keep calm at all times. There's no point in blowing a fuse and retaliating, risking the chance of losing your high grade totty. All that banter and hard work gone in one meeting with the parent. It is only natural they want to protect their babies from sexual predators like us. Go with it.

#59 ALWAYS NOTICE A NEW HAIRCUT

Even if she's not had her hair done, it's a good idea just to say 'Have you had your hair cut it looks different, it looks nice'. Even if she's bald.

A tip: If someone has had a perm never say 'I like your perm.' It's supposed to look natural. So you could say 'Your perm looks natural, that can't be a perm. That's a perm? No way!'

#60 AVOID THE PAINTERS

When a girl has PMT go out with your mates, or tell her you have a illness that is holding you hostage to your bed. You can't move. Stay away! Nothing you can say will fix anything, you will always be in the wrong and could be risking physical damage to your mind the PMT version of girl you fell for. It's of nonsensical spouts. when someone has to caught vampire. It their ass!

body and soul. Remember your girlfriend is not the just a beautiful shell full It's like on vampire films kill their loved one who has is not them! Just stake

If for some avoid them, anything they helmet and or clothing.

reason you can't just agree and do say and wear a other protective

He knows it. Still got his shoes on too for a speedy getaway.

#61 UNDERSTAND WHAT SHE MEANS WHEN SHE SAYS...

When you've been going out with yer bird for a while you'll realise that what she says in't always what she means. Here's a few common translations to give you an idea.

1. I'm tired, I'm gonna go to bed

I'm tired I'm gonna go to bed, I'll be asleep by the time you've locked up. Don't start sticking it in my back cos you're not getting any.

2. Shall we have a quiet night in tonight babe?

I don't wanna go out tonight cos I've got nowt to wear.

3. Hey have you cut your hair?

What have you trimmed ya pubes for?
Doesn't make you knob look any bigger.
In fact now it looks like a little boy's willy.

4. Do you like it when I do that?

God how long is this gonna take? My arm is killing me.

And girls, life's a bit simpler with us fellas but there is usually a bit of stuff we don't say but is obvious. Just in case, here's a few common translations for you too:

1. I'm tired, I'm gonna go to bed

I'm pretty tired but I still want anything sexual you wanna offer to me.

2. Shall we have a quiet night in tonight babe?

We haven't had sex for ages, why don't we get a take out and then have sex.

3. Hey you've cut your hair. Its nice.

What have you done to your barnet? You've made yerself look like a boy.

4. Do you like it when I do that?

I'm good at sex aren't I!

#62 NEVER FORGET A VALENTINE'S DAY CARD

It comes round every year. It's horrible if you're spending it alone (that's what they tell me) and its horrible when you're with someone. The harassment of having to take them out, everywhere is double the price and fully booked. Getting them flowers and a card and all that junk. But you have to do it. It makes them feel good and in return you will be credited with blow jobs. So uncle Keith is gonna help you. Simply cut along the perforated lines.

Here's one I made earlier

Happy Valen

CUT

FOLD

FOLD

Relationship

OOSH!

Happy Valentine

CUT

Dear.....

Fanks for being my valentine person

You are the fittest girl in't world

I want to bang you till it burns
and just ignore the pain and
keep going some more.

I truly believe I will never
get bored of you.

All't best

U
O
S
H
!

#63 CELEBRATE VALENTINE'S DAY IN STYLE

Because most places will be full with hopeless romantics being duped by the whole Valentine's consumerist thing (use that – the commercialisation of love is sad, isn't it? It'll make you look proper sensitive). Get a suchi cook book, leave it out on't counter. Pick up some suchi from somewhere. Set it out nice on't table making sure to discard all packaging. Light a couple of candles on't table. Put the same music on in't background as when you first pumped her. Tell her that you've been having lessons in cooking suchi especially for today and that her gift is between your legs with a bow tied around it.

Simple.

And girls, for the fella in yer life on Valentine's Day... Don't bother with any flowers. Take him down t' boozer. Bring him back to yours pissed as arseholes. Tell him he can do anything he wants to you. If you're not in't mood by the time you've slipped into something more provocative or just yer jim-jams he'll be in the land of nod before you can say you've got a headache. In the morning tell him that he was amazing. He'll go to work feeling good about himself whilst you can go shopping with the girls. Everyone's a winner!

#64 REMEMBER TO BUY REGULAR GIFTS

pissy whiff

1. Chocolates are an oldy but goody but they aren't cheap. And if yer girlfriend is a fat fighter you're gonna be helping no-one.

2. Get her some flowers, again they aren't cheap but they work a treat. Most flowers smell of piss but women love them. Daffodils can easily be picked up from the park for free. Tell her they are the colour of sunshine and she is the sunshine in your heart.

3. 'Keith Lemon's Fit' on DVD. Normally buying a girl a work out DVD might come across a bit rude as it suggests she's put a bit of beef on. But not this one. Its not a proper work out DVD. But it'll get your right arm looking like Popeye's! There's plenty of bang tidy birds in it. So actually perhaps don't give this to your girlfriend – just keep it for yerself.

4. 'Keith Lemon's Very Brilliant World Tour' DVD. This is a really fun educational documentary about me travelling around the world discovering different cultures. Tell her you wanna take her off on a gap year fingy.

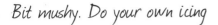

Bit mushy. Do your own icing

OSH!

5. One of those small beer fridges with her favourite brand of beer printed on the glass door. Ace!

6. A Rabbit vibrators fingy. They've come down in price now, they're about £35. Leave her with that and go down 't pub with yer mates.

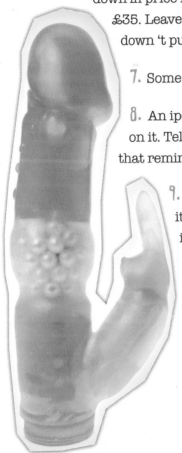

7. Some Ann Summers vouchers.

8. An ipod thing with some romantic tunes on it. Tell her you've uploaded all the tunes that remind you of her. Bang!

9. Any 'Sex in t' City' DVD. I don't like it myself as it gives women too many ideas.

10. One of this large cookies with a sexy message on, something like 'I would destroy you'.

And for the lads, ladies take a look at these goodies:

1. 3D telly. Ace!

2. Nintendo 3D fingy

3. Ipad 2

4. Xbox, Playstation, Wee or all of them

5.. 'Keith Lemon's Fit' on DVD. Like I said its funny and its got lots of totty in it

6. 'Keith Lemon's Very Brilliant World Tour' DVD. Just looks nice on't shelf next to 'Keith Lemon's Fit'. Looks like he's got the complete set

7. A segway - completely versatile and consistently enjoyable

8. Some snakeskin cowboy boots and a snakeskin jacket

9. A trip to space with Richard Branson

10. Moustache

This is an ace gift

You can cut out the one opposite for free

MOUSTACHE TO CUT OUT

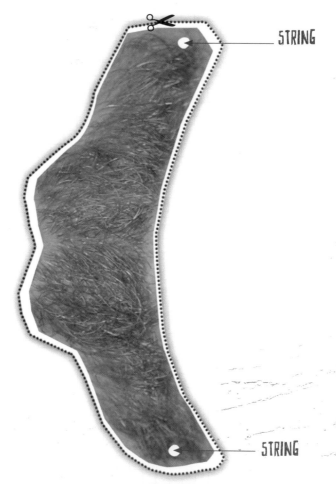

STRING

STRING

Maybe Richard Branson is me dad. Been
told I look like him as well. Can't really be
a virgin cos if he is then he can't be me dad

#65 IF IT ISN'T WORKING OUT, GET RID

Never a nice thing: always awkward and horrible, especially if they start crying.
But sometimes it has to be done and the best thing is to let her down gently.
Here are a few ideas. Use one of these to get straight to the point and outta there.

- It's not you it's your breasts.
  They're too small for my hands.

- It's not your breasts it's my hands, they're too big.

- I am a hormone sexual.

- It's not me it's you. I don't like ya anymore.

- It's going nowhere. You want one fing and I want another and they're both two different fings. I wish we didn't both want two different fings. It's so upsetting but it's for the best otherwise both of us are gonna have two fings we just don't want.

- In another time and place I think we could've had a beautiful thing. But in this time and place its just ugly as fuck.

I always keep a one way ticket to China from Leeds handy

Don't be afraid to dump!

- I can't put all my time into you that you deserve. Me mam is sick and her eyes have fallen out. So I'm gonna have to be at home for a long time being me mam's eyes.

- If I was a bit older I'd love to take this further but I'm just not emotionally mature enough to handle this. I wanna see more of my mates down t' park.

- I'm just not good enough for you. You deserve better. I don't wanna hold ya back.

- I'm moving to China. I don't think its fair to expect you to come with me. They don't even speak English, I can't expect you to come with me and live in a place where nobody will understand what yer saying when you might be asking for something as simple as directions for the toilet. You can't just stand there and crap ya pants.

One of those will surely be fitting to your predicament. Nice one.

#66 GET TWO TELLIES

I think when you do move in with someone you both have to respect each others habit's but it is a good idea to have two tellys. You don't wanna be stuck in a room all night having to watch A Place in the Sun if Back to the Future is on the other side.

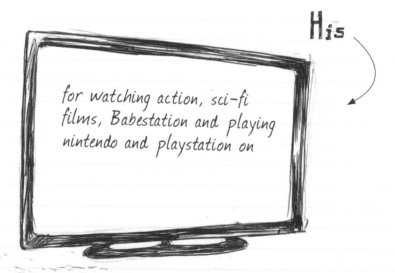

His

for watching action, sci-fi films, Babestation and playing nintendo and playstation on

Hers

for watching a place in the sun, eastenders, corrie and booking holidays on't teletext

NEVER REVEAL THE NUMBER

Whatever you do, never tell her the real number of birds you've banged. It's not gonna help anyone. If she insists then use the golden formula:

Real number divided by your age, minus the age of the oldest girl you've had.

(unless she's 84 otherwise you'll be in minus figures)

#68 MAINTAIN YOUR INDEPENDENCE

I've had many woman ask to marry me... in't street, on tweeter, in clubs. If that does happen the nicest way to decline I find is to simply laugh and say 'That is so sweet'.

I've seen so many lads just throw their lives away getting married. No longer can they do owt without getting a pink slip from their missus saying they can do owt. Me? I can do what I want when I want. Just at the drop of the hat, if I wanna go to Blackpool for the weekend with the lads or even furtherer (Wales - some fit birds there) I can. So if you do get yerself in a spot of bother, the key is to maintain your independence.

By the way if you're that fit Welsh bird I had in a caravan, think your name was butter tits and you're reading this then you know who you are and I know who you are. If you fancy a sequel to what happened that night that'll be bigger, better and longer than before, come down to the Celebrity Juice studios in London.

#69 IF YOU GET DUMPED, GO ON T' REBOUND

Its horrible when it happens, I imagine. Your heart brock into a million pieces, your pride shat on all over the floor, the rejection. It must be horrible. But if you do play like you're brock some girls actually like that. If you get lucky you could get the ear of a good listener that likes to physically fix fings. She'll help you forget about all your problems.

Some people spend their whole life being the rebound and have very healthy sex lives. Being the rebound is no bad fing. It can mean you can get some tidy totty that would normally be out of your league. Result!

For example Jay Z and Beyonce... Surely she was on the rebound from some one else. He's got dollars but he's no oil painting, whereas Beyonce = stupid fit! She should be arrested. I'd let her kick the crap out of me.

Get your pulling radar back on straight way and switch it to FULL POWER!

THAT'S IT

P.s. I apologise for any bad spelling and grammar I am 47% dislexic.

Hopefully this little book has or will help you to be a suc-sex. Be confident but not predatory and it won't be long before you're getting exactly what you want. You will be a better person for reading this – but before you unleash yerself onto the world, do the quiz opposite to test what you've learnt. If you can't answer these questions, you're a dingbat. Go back to page 1 and read the book again.

And ladies, I'm sorry I didn't write much from a female perspective but I don't know everything about the female mind as I pee standing up. But I love you all. If I had the time I would have it off with all of you. Fat, fin, black, white, cream – I'd do you all.

Fanks for reading this. If I don't see ya through t' week I'll see ya through t' window.

Big up to the United States of Leeds!

All t'best

Kevin Lennon

P.s. etc. I promised you some girls numbers to call if you have no luck out there.

P.p.s. There's a good chance that Billy Ocean could be me dad – him who sang 'When the going gets tough'. Me mam said she had a fing with him. So big shout out to me dad. Fanks for having it off with me mam. Without you I'd never be here.

NAME *Suzy (From Liverpool. Proper up for a laugh will do owt and I mean owt)*
PHONE *07024 56327*

NAME *Sharon (Rich girl, fit and posh)*
PHONE *03486 284571*

NAME *Cloe and Zoe (blond twins, big bangers. One of them has a lazy eye)*
PHONE *07984 45672*

WHAT HAVE YOU LEARNT?

1 If you're working on your style, who should you look to for inspiration?
   a. Owen Wilson, Nicky Clarke and Simon le Bon
   b. Johnny Depp, Brad Pitt and Orlando Bloom
   c. Robert Pattinson, Zac Efron and Taylor Lautner

2 What should you spray on your body?
   a. Nothing. Only woolly woofter's like getting sprayed
   b. Fake tan to make you look like a stud
   c. Deoderiser

3 What shoes should you wear to impress the ladies?
   a. Snakeskin shoes
   b. Cowboy boots
   c. Jellies

4 What should you do every day?
   a. Have a wank and learn a new word
   b. Trim your nose hair
   c. Eat 11 pieces of fruit and veg

5 How do you pull in a soft play area?
   a. Borrow a mates kid. There's bound to be a milf on a dad hunt
   b. Put a couple of those plastic balls down your leather trousers
   c. Dress up like a lost kid

6 If you've got a face like a pig, what should you do?
   a. Celebrate it - beauty is in t'eye of beholder
   b. Wear large sunglasses
   c. Hang around with someone who looks a troll - you'll look fit in comparison

7 Girls, what vibe should you send out?
   a. Sensitive and after emotional support
   b. One of the lads but with bangers
   c. Fat as well as fick

8 Lads, what vibe should you send out?
   a. Hard on't outside, soft and juicy on't inside
   b. Soft on't outside, hard on't inside
   c. Soft everywhere but the tallywacker. Ooosh!

9 Which one is the best chat up line?
  a. 'What makes you tick?'
  b. 'If I had the chance to rearrange the alphabet, I would put U and I together and sex you up till it hurt me'
  c. 'Can I buy you a drink?'

10 How do you get a girl in the mood?
  a. Champagne and oysters
  b. A scotch egg and half a bottle of zambooka
  c. Tea and digestives

11 When having a one-night stand. You should...
  a. Do a shit in the corner of the room
  b. Do a song that you've learned in ya head
  c. Not hold back. Trap two and all

12 Why do girls like lads who love animals?
  a. If you can make her kitten purr, she'll trust you to smash her back doors in
  b. It makes them fink you'll be a good parent
  c. If you can afford all that pet food, then you must be dead rich

13 Which of the following is a playground flirtation?
  a. 'You're carrying a bit of timber, aren't ya. Looking good for it though
  b. You're F.A.F you are. Will you blow me?
  c. The elbow grope

14 Who is Chanelle?
  a. Victoria Beckham
  b. Chantelle Houghton
  c. Chanelle Hayes

15 If you get mixed up with a co-worker, you should
  a. Tell her she's dreamt the whole thing. Dingbat
  b. Send an all company email with all the details
  c. Only get frisky after a few gins

16 Why should you meet her mates?
  a. You'll see what they love about her, so you'll love her even more
  b. Tidy birds hang out with other tidy birds. Fact.
  c. She wants you to, and you'll do as she ruddy well says, there's a good lad

17 What do you say to yer girl to make her happy?
a. 'Have you had your hair cut it looks different, it looks nice.' Even if she's bald
b. 'Let the tash see the gash'
c. 'I love you with more than just me balls'

18 What should you get her for Valentine's Day?
a. Suchi
b. Raw chicken
c. Cockolate: Cock-shaped chocolate

19 What should you get him for Valentine's Day?
a. Two tickets to go down Flower Show
b. Clippers for his tash
c. Snakeskin boots

20 If it in't working out, what do you say?
a. 'It's not you, it's me'
b. 'It's not me, it's you. I don't like ya anymore'
c. Nothing. Just switch off yer phone and if you see her pretend you've lost yer voice.

RESULTS:

0-6: Maybe you should try sausage smoking, which is fine by me. Or do what my mate Terry did and go and live up a holy mountain.

7-15: Good effort, but you'll only be busy three nights a week. You need to read the rules again with one of them bright yellow penlighter thingy's.

16-20: Even if you look like Cameron David, you'll be banging tidy birds till the cow's come home... Nice one.

An Orion paperback
First published in Great Britain in 2011
by Orion
This paperback edition published in 2014
by Orion Books Ltd,
Orion House, 5 Upper St Martin's Lane,
London WC2H 9EA

An Hachette UK Company

1 3 5 7 9 10 8 6 4 2

A CIP catalogue record for this book is available from the British Library.

ISBN 978 1 4091 3780 1

Printed and bound in Thailand by Imago

Design: Brian Roberts
Art Direction: Helen Ewing
Editorial: Jane Sturrock

The Orion Publishing Group's policy is to use papers that are natural,
renewable and recyclable and made from wood grown in sustainable forests.
The logging and manufacturing processes are expected to conform to the
environmental regulations of the country of origin.

Every effort has been made to fulfil requirements with regard to reproducing
copyright material. The author and the publisher will be glad to rectify any
omissions at the earliest opportunity.

www.orionbooks.co.uk

PICTURE CREDITS:

Rex Features: 2, 10, 16, 23 (right), 119, 139

Getty Images: 12, 15, 18, 19, 21 (right), 22-3, 29 (both), 31, 33, 34, 40, 41, 42, 43, 47, 48,
50, 53, 58, 72 (both), 75 (right), 77, 86, 94, 97 (both), 98, 102, 105, 108, 114, 120, 123,
129, 131

Big Pictures: 27

Leigh Francis: 17, 21(bottom), 24, 32, 44, 54 (right), 55-7, 65, 71, 88, 99, 110, 126,
133, 139

Richard Chambury / Richfoto: 54 (left), 55, 61, 80

Brian Roberts: 107, 118-9

istockphoto: 75 (left), 122, 132